*Getting Through the Night*

Old Ironsides

FROM THE LIBRARY OF

To Brenda,
    This book helped us so much
after Paul died & I have shared
it with several friends. Hope it
helps you, too in the coming weeks.
            Hugs & Daisies,
            Jim & Paula

*Books by Eugenia Price*

FICTION
Margaret's Story
Maria
Don Juan McQueen
The Beloved Invader
New Moon Rising
Lighthouse

NONFICTION
Getting Through the Night
At Home on St. Simons
Diary of a Novel
St. Simons Memoir
No Pat Answers
Leave Yourself Alone
Learning to Live from The Acts
Learning to Live from The Gospels
The Unique World of Women
Just as I Am
Make Love Your Aim
The Wider Place
God Speaks to Women Today
What Is God Like?
Find Out for Yourself
A Woman's Choice
Beloved World
Woman to Woman
Share My Pleasant Stones
Early Will I Seek Thee
Never a Dull Moment
The Burden Is Light
Discoveries

Eugenia Price

# Getting Through the Night

*Finding Your Way*
*After the Loss*
*of a Loved One*

The Dial Press
New York

Published by
The Dial Press
1 Dag Hammarskjold Plaza
New York, New York 10017

Copyright © 1982 by Eugenia Price
All rights reserved.
Manufactured in the United States of America
Second Printing
Design by Francesca Belanger

Library of Congress Cataloging in Publication Data

Price, Eugenia.
    Getting through the night.

    1. Consolation.   2. Grief.   I. Title.
BV4905.2.P73          248.8'6          81-17390
ISBN 0-385-27658-3                    AACR2

*For Nelldeane, Susan, Burney, Jeanne, Rosa Maude, Ruby, Myron, Bob, and Don—all of whom allowed me to share their journey into morning.*

*. . . and after this book was written, I must include Millie Price, who just lost my wonderful brother, Joe.*

## Contents

*"Weeping may endure for a night,*
*but joy cometh in the morning."*

Psalms 30:5b

ONE

*Getting Through*
*the Night*

$M$ost of us greet a bright, cloudless day with a cheer.

Most of us, at one time or another, fear the dark. Oh, nights can be beautiful if our world spins along upright, if those we love are nearby, if we are in a familiar, safe place. As long as there are friends and family and lovers with us, we stand in the special silence a night brings and wonder at the stars; the moon rides high, silver as a coin, or rises copper and heavy out of dark water—or the branches of a pine tree. We can actually look at the moon, the stars— our eyes can bear that. Not so the sun. Still, the sun gives light and when there is light to see, we are less afraid.

But if the person who made the moon lovelier,

the sun more golden, in your world has gone, whether by death or divorce or any other drastic change, do you wonder, cry aloud: "Will this night ever end? Will I ever get through it?"

If you are in a long night, these pages are for you. Perhaps you can read them only one or two at a time, but they are for *you.* If you have not yet entered that long night, the book is for you, too. The way through any shadowy place is always less confusing if we have even one small idea of what to expect— one tiny glimmer of light.

Nights can be wondered over, marveled about— *but they are dark.* And unless we are complete, happy, untroubled, they can be dread- and fear-filled, simply because of the darkness.

At night we don't see things as they are. The shapes of trees and flower gardens and houses, even on moonlit nights, distort before our eyes because we cannot take in their true dimensions. We are able to see by night-light only the portions of familiar objects not erased by shadow and blackness. In the dark the shape of a familiar bush or shrub moving ever so slightly in a night breeze can appear a threat—can trip a mysterious lever in our minds so that the very bush we may have planted with our own hands appears shadowy, unknown, sinister.

Not only do shapes loom in the dark; sounds intensify. A giant oak or elm limb, settling for the night in cooler air, may sound like a strange footstep. A branch may brush our window all day without our hearing it, but the same branch, scraping against a window in the darkness, can stop our hearts. At age six or sixty, we cry out for the light, for the safety it offers; because with it, we can *see* around us.

Nights have always come as regularly as days. In a sense, they should not be unfamiliar to us, but when the familiar, harmonious patterns of our life have just been shredded, nights can be the very worst times of all. When a beloved one is suddenly gone— nights seem to make the loss unbearable. "If I can just manage to get through the *first night* alone," we cry, without husband, without wife, without child, friend or parent. . . . Night *has* always come as regularly as day, but it so changes the familiar that we fear getting lost in it.

The aching heart can somehow survive peopled, light-filled days. Darkness has long been the symbol of loneliness, of being lost; the symbol of danger, of dread, of weeping.

"Weeping may endure for a *night*. . . ."

If you have lost someone, if a part of your very

life has been chopped off by that loss, you do not need an exposition on the horrors of a long night of weeping, of waiting—in the dark—for morning to come. You already know.

We have the word of God that He knows, too: "Weeping may endure for a night. . . ."

Does it help that God knows about our nights of weeping?

Yes, but not enough. Desperately we need to know that the hard, grinding work of grieving will somehow, sometime, end. Will I ever smile again because I *feel* like smiling and not just to make my poor, patient friends feel better about me? Will I ever learn to live without him? Without her? Will I ever be a whole person again? *Will this long night ever end?*

God says that it will.

The missing will go on, but the hard work of grieving, the darkness, the agony, *will end.* You can be whole again. It won't seem possible now, perhaps, but because God is a Redeemer God, there *will* someday—for you—be "beauty for [these] ashes." There will be "joy for the oil of mourning."

Joy? Yes.

"Weeping may endure for a night, but joy cometh in the morning."

Did God really mean that the grieving heart can know *joy* again?

He did. He does. But the joy about which God speaks is far deeper than what we think of as happiness. There is as much difference between God's joy and human happiness as between night and day. For some of us, once our night has ended, this joy can be an entirely new, never-before-realized experience.

In my novel *Maria* there is this line: "Joy is God in the marrow of your bones."

Whether you know God or not, in the present darkness of your grief His promise that ". . . joy cometh in the morning" may sound ludicrous, even cruel. It is neither. It is fact. And if you don't know Him, or if you feel shut off from Him, read anyway, because He knows you completely—*as you are this minute*. He is "acquainted with all your ways."

For you to begin to know Him, to sense His presence again, requires only a swift turning of your inner being toward His.

"Come unto me," Jesus said, "and I will give you rest." Who needs rest more than you right now, if your heart is worn out by grief?

"I am the light of the world." Who needs light

more than you while the night of weeping endures? Who has more need of morning?

One thing is clear: There is no promise anywhere of a magic wand to end grief. But we do have God's word for it that anyone willing to try—even a little—to understand that there is a way into morning will make it through that night. If we know anything at all about the nature of God, of His intentions toward us, we can, for now, lay hold of the fact of morning. The night of weeping has no set number of hours. Its length depends in many ways upon our trying to grasp the *fact* that even our night can end.

This small book is meant to help you take at least one step toward your morning. You will find no doctrinaire, crisp, pat answers here. There are so many kinds of grief—so many variations within those kinds—that no single book could cover them. These pages have a single purpose: to give anyone who, for whatever reasons, is in grief, an assurance that there is help available—God's help—and that even the smallest *participation* in His promised healing can bring the morning more swiftly. Death is not the only reason for grief. There are as many kinds of losses as there are people and no two are alike. Here we will attempt to show that God is dependable *in grief* always—no matter what causes it—and that once we *accept* the loss, there is a chance for participation in healing for the stricken person left behind.

Are you rebelling already at that word *accept*? To accept the irrevocable fact that a loved one is gone, whether by natural death, desertion, divorce, suicide, or accident is the first necessity. But in the early hours of our journey through any darkness, true acceptance is often impossible. You will say, "You don't need to remind me that my loved one is gone. It hurts to breathe." But true acceptance does not stop with mere acknowledgment of the fact. True acceptance, when one is counting on God's redemption of grief, *includes* our agreement to join God in bringing an end to our night of weeping. And you who grieve, only you, will know when the moment comes that you feel you *can* begin to participate with Him.

If you are reading this while your loss is fresh and bitter, quite probably all you can take in now is that the time will come when you will know. One friend wrote: "For days I just walked around in the yard where we'd worked together for so long and said aloud to myself, with no sense of speaking to God: 'What will I do? What will happen to me?' "

This is not being self-centered. This is being human. Those days of stark desperation must be worked through. Grieving is work. Hard work. And so, often, our first almost unconscious act of participation must be to accept ourselves in that beginning traumatic stage and feel no guilt for seeming to be so helpless, so faithless, so self-concerned. The pain is still too sharp. Our bodies as well as our minds may be in shock. We are not to blame for this. We are human. To expect anyone who has loved to walk away from an open grave in good, strong spirits—no matter how deeply rooted faith is—is as ridiculous as to expect a patient to get up off an operating table after major surgery and walk away.

The single purpose of this book is to attempt to get your attention, if you are in grief, long enough to plant somewhere in your mind the *fact* that God does promise that your night of weeping can end. He does not promise that you will be unscarred as though you had never loved; He does not promise that you will ever stop missing, or even hurting. He promises that, in His strength, you can one day learn to live again in morning light.

❦

Grief confuses, exhausts, seems to block the mind from thinking. God knows this. He created our minds. He knows far better than we what they can do. He also knows what they can't understand.

And so, while the length of the night of weeping does depend upon our beginning to understand that God has every intention of bringing us into morning again, *the responsibility for that miracle is His*—that is for Him to do. He is completely willing, even eager, to shoulder the heaviest part of the understanding needed in the early, darkest hours.

How can we be sure of this? Once more, we have His word for it. God says of Himself: "I *am* understanding." He isn't prodding you into feeling better by reminding you that He has the ability to understand human grief, He is stating another more awesome fact. He is succinctly characterizing Himself to you: "I *am* understanding."

To *be* understanding is far more than merely to *have* it. Which means that no matter how thick your darkness, how hopeless your heart, God is in the midst of it—*being understanding*. You can do nothing to change that. Nothing. You can cry out that you hate Him. The understanding will not change, will not even waver, because God *is* understanding and He cannot change.

"Weeping may endure for a night. . . ." He knows that. No one on earth understands your weeping as He does.

". . . but joy cometh in the morning." It does? Yes.

Morning *can* come for you. For me. For anyone who truly wants it again. It will come for anyone who can manage even the smallest understanding that, because of God's very nature, because of His dreams and plans for us, we can be whole again. Whole in a way we never were, because as we stumble through our grief, *receiving* from Him, we will be added to from the eternal stuff of creation itself.

There will come a time when you realize that you no longer want to clutch your grief as though to let it go would rob you of the last thing you have left of your loved one. God understands that to do this is a normal human reaction. He will wait for you to be willing to let go.

These pages are here for you to *use*—in whatever hour of your night—even one sentence, one paragraph, at a time. What is here has helped other grieving hearts, including my own; has given definite rays of light—hope that the "night of weeping"

*11*

will end. They are not here for you to use in the foolish hope that you can stifle your grief. Grieving, if one has loved, is a part of life.

But morning can come for you, so that, in a brand-new way, you can emerge into it not only a better, more sensitive, more aware person, but capable, as perhaps you have never been, of experiencing and giving—joy.

First, there are important, creative things to consider. . . .

TWO

# Coping
## with Time

"*T*ime is a period set apart in some specified or implied way from others." That is an accepted definition of an interval of time and true as far as it goes. I find it strikingly inadequate here.

When hours seem endless, they are not "set apart." They are simply blurred and endless. Time can be the source, to the grieving heart, of the heaviest pain: "How can I face all those nights up ahead? The decisions *time* will bring—without him? Without her? How can I just go on living days and weeks (measures of time) doing the things I have to do in this new, strange, empty, shocking time? Grief time. The time in my life when I am no longer myself."

Memories may be the whetstone that brings to grief its sharpest edge. Someone will mention or you

will read of a particular year—1938, 1956, 1975—
and the thrust of new pain will seem unbearable.
Mention of a certain year can empty the heart of all
hope of recovery: A love song came out that year, a
book read aloud with the one now gone. A son grad-
uated from college, a daughter's wedding took place
back in one certain year when life was still all of a
piece. Sunsets, shared for so long—beauty reveled
in together—can now be all pain. Time, measured,
as man must, by calendars and clocks, becomes a
tormentor. Especially when it crawls past, one empty
minute following another.

*How will I ever learn to cope with time?*

*Can* I ever learn to cope with time again?

If it is true that "with God all things are possible,"
yes, you can. I can. But repeating that fragment of
Scripture when the knife of memory stabs probably
won't help. Not at once, anyway. The day can come,
unless you are refusing to allow God's help, when
you will suddenly realize that nothing *was* impossible with Him after all. Yet, during the time in
which your grief is fresh (and it always stays "fresh"
far longer than our friends realize), hearing someone remind you that "with God all things are possible" *can* fill you with bitterness. Nothing, *nothing*
that has ever happened since the world began, could

have been as hard as your grief! Maybe all other things are possible with God—not this, not this.

No human being—no other human being on earth—can understand the *weight* of your burden. But here is the key: God does understand the exact extent and pain of your grief because He created *you* in the first place—*as you are*. He didn't create you as someone else is; He created you as you are. Say aloud to Him this minute: "Thou knowest my downsitting and mine uprising, thou understandest my thought afar off. Thou compassest my path and my lying down, and art acquainted with *all my ways*."

Psalm 139: 1-3

And remember that this Creator God says of Himself where *you* are concerned: "I am understanding."

To understand you and your suffering is God's very nature.

You see, to God, your morning is already here. You have already endured the weeping night. Does this help? Not unless we can open ourselves to one small ray of light—light that alone can bring us understanding. Not understanding of *why* the loved one died; not understanding of how suddenly to throw open the blinds and welcome the new day. Rather, understanding of the Creator God's intentions—His plans for us when our hearts are smashed. Never think that God moves by learned techniques. He attends us according to what He already knows about us as individuals and this guarantees His patience with us.

Some of His followers seem able to throw off sorrow or failure or disappointment, shout "Praise the Lord!" and go blithely on. Well, He understands about them, too, but "getting through the night" usually takes time. Often, one hour at a time. A wise, older friend once said to me, "Get through this hour. Don't worry about the next." God is saying that to you: "Get through this hour. I'll be in the next hour with you and I will understand exactly how you feel in it."

God does understand our nights, but His intentions for us in the long run have to do with morning. With the "joy [that] cometh in the morning." Does joy seem out of reach to you now? If it does, God knows all about it; but think about this: Isn't freedom from this pain what you want more than anything? Don't you cry out for the pain to end? Isn't this what you really want? Then, can you grasp, however weakly, the tip end of the truth that God *can* bring about your relief? Your *morning* most certainly is God's will. If it isn't, then Jesus was confused when He said that He came to earth to get into the weeping with us so that we could have "a more abundant life."

Do you think He was confused? Or lying? Or holding out something that you alone can never reach? Does the thought of an abundant life again—ever—for you seem impossible? No one understands better than God if it does. After all, Jesus did come to earth as one of us. Even when He knew He would raise His beloved friend Lazarus from the dead in minutes, He wept. "Jesus wept." To you, right now, that short sentence could be the most important verse in the entire Bible.

God is not disappointed in you for weeping, for feeling that you can never be whole again. He knows you. He knows exactly how that stretch of empty time up ahead appears to you now. Jesus was weeping for His lost friend, but He was also weeping because of pain in His own heart at the sight of such grief in the eyes of Lazarus's two sisters. Jesus is weeping over you now—even though He knows of your morning to come. He is weeping even though He has that morning ready for you at this minute. It is ready—but unlike so many of our well-meaning friends who seem taken aback when we don't latch on to their offered Scripture texts and bounce back,

God understands. He understands the way in which a little more time can give you a chance to make your way through the early shock. He has your morning ready, He could lead you right into it, but He knows you can't follow—quite yet.

He lives right now in eternity, where time does not exist, but all that could be contained of God in a human being did visit our planet and was trapped in time—for thirty-three years, as we reckon it. He knows what it's like for you, trapped also in time, facing years ahead without your loved one. He understands how endless it seems to you this minute to have to wait for some nebulous "morning" to come. I don't believe for an instant that He had to enter human time in order to find out what it was like. I believe with all my heart that He did it so that *we would know that He knows*. We do not cry out to some remote, half-attentive deity when we cry out to Christ. Everything He did—from His birth in a stable to His ugly death on a cross—He did so that we would know that He knows.

Still, safe passage through your night of weeping is an accomplished fact for Jesus Christ, because He, like your loved one, is no longer caught in time.

Think about that.

God is not trapped in time and neither is your

loved one. And yet both can remember, can, at this moment, understand, identify with the fact that you are still time-bound. They know. Your loved one knows about you now, as does God. This is not a theory of mine. Paul wrote: ". . . absent from the body, present with the Lord." John, who lived so close to Jesus on earth, wrote: ". . . it doth not yet appear what we shall be: but we know that . . . *we shall be like him;* for we shall see him as he is." Your loved one *sees* God as He really is. Not as our numerous and distorted human concepts have made Him seem to be.

Let this become a part of you: Your loved one and God know what a wrenching experience it was for you to wake up this morning and realize, all over again, the dark reality of your grief. They know how desolate your table seems and why you eat by a window from a tray now. They know how hard it is to swallow. How deafening the silence is around you. How long the night. They know that well-meaning friends, at times, only added to your exhaustion in the first days after the loss. They also know, now, that many of those friends have gotten busy with their own lives again, so that meaningless hours stretch ahead—for you.

Your loved one, with God, knows. But don't

make the common mistake of worrying that if your
loved one knows of your agony, your endless hours,
it will cause him or her anxiety. Concern, yes. The
love not only goes on, it is free at last to increase
forever. But worry? Anxiety? No. Because your
loved one now has the mind of God and knows exactly how this is all going to come out for you. As
God knows. They know that one day, you will turn
that corner so that you can begin to *use* the very
hours that now seem only to be *abusing* you.

Time is a trap for us on earth, but it is also our
only means of measuring the way out. We would
have no idea at all how to live without time. Try to
keep clear that God *is* understanding—and now, so
is your loved one. He or she is no longer impatient
with you. No one is saying "Hurry up." God and
your loved one can also remember what it is like to
be time-bound. They and everyone who has ever
entered the eternal presence are with you in this.
Coping with time today—tonight—isn't your work
alone. There is "a cloud of witnesses."

The Quaker philosopher Thomas Kelley wrote
of "the Eternal Now."

The eternal *now*.

Don't try to grasp that all at once. Give yourself some time to think about it. Try not to make things harder for yourself by fretting, because time is measured like knots tied in a stretched-out string. I find that I can divert myself from dreading the approach of a certain time that can bring me pain by stopping to look at some small beauty. "But seeing beautiful things hurts too much!" Still, one small instant of *focused awareness* can bring immeasurable relief.

My late, wise, very human friend Gladys Taber wrote in her book on grief, *Another Path:* "By observing, my eyes saw the mysterious light of dawn and the still blaze of noon [again]. I looked at the world—and I forgot myself. I began to find some good in every day. I didn't try to work at being happy, I worked at finding that good (that beauty) in every day and experiencing it fully. And, at night, I thanked God in my prayers for whatever the good had been. It might be any one of a number of things: an unexpected telephone call from a friend. A letter of warm appreciation for something I had written. A neighbor dropping in with a bouquet of pansies from her greenhouse in midwinter. The overnight blossoming of the lilies of the valley. The voice of my granddaughter trying to get her tongue around words. 'Tzeez,' she says triumphantly, meaning 'cheese.' "

As you would stop to rest a short while in the midst of a hard physical job, so we can give ourselves tiny moments of rest from grieving by willing ourselves to focus—just for a moment—on some small cheerful sound or sunny sight not directly related to our grief. The darkness may flood back before a full minute has passed, but relief will have happened, too.

There are no words to explain "the eternal now." Your loved one and God live in it. We don't yet, but *we can dip in*—during those willed moments of awareness.

Planning ahead (in time) may have been your way of living until now. Of course, a certain amount of thought must be given to the future. But when the loneliness and emptiness of that future seem to roll back onto *now*—stop. Stop *in time* exactly where you are and give yourself a chance to realize—something. To recognize—something. Even if it is only a sun spot on the wall, the mystery of an invisible breeze moving a branch outside—your own two hands. Give thanks for the smallest realization, the tiniest recognition. This is progress.

Appreciate your hands, your home, that neighbor

23

who helped so much just by being near. Your family, your children, your church—the sky, trees, one particular river. Give thanks for them. If, as with some, you have no family, no children, your way into morning could be shortened, because aloneness cuts the surest, shortest path through the tangle to God Himself. If there is no human being nearby to hold our hand, we may offer it more readily to God.

God is a Person. He is not merely an immutable law of the universe. No mere law could promise to be "with you always."

Say anything to Him. Anything at all. "Even in the first stage of grief, my heart was eased when I prayed," Gladys Taber wrote. Knowing Gladys, I'm sure those first prayers were not in measured English.

God "hears" our thoughts—the bitter thoughts and the grateful ones. What He longs for is that we *recognize* that He hears and is standing by, ready to lead, when He knows we can follow, into the morning already prepared for us.

THREE

*Concentrate*
*on Your Loved One*

You are already thinking of your loved one anyway. This is natural. You can't miss someone you aren't thinking of. That your every moment is shot through with reminders is as much a natural part of life as is death. We speak of "what comes naturally," and generally we think of something natural with us as being easy. This is not always true. Birth is natural, illness is natural, failure is natural, grief is natural—none is easy.

It is natural, to be expected, that your mind is—however painfully—most of the time on the one who has just gone away. Well, if God is a Redeemer God, and He is, He can make redemptive *use* of that for you. You can't help thinking of him, of her, so is there a way that this mental preoccupation can be helpful? Can be used?

Yes.

You miss so much. You miss the letters, the key in the door, the laughter, the small confidences, the meeting of minds. You even miss the complaints, the grumblings, the miffed or indifferent grunts from behind the sports pages. You miss—you are only half present yourself, because that person is absent. You think about him—you think about her—all day long. All night long.

This is fact, so can't the missing be turned just a little, even for the length of one minute, so that it can be experienced another way? A more creative way? Even if you have to pretend—or if it seems like pretending—try. Any small effort on your part, to begin to allow God to make some kind of creative, redemptive *use* of your pain, can start you on the road to that promised "joy [that] cometh in the morning."

Right now that word "joy" may choke you, but don't stop reading. More than any human being can understand, God understands why you're choked at the very mention of "joy" at a time of such pain.

For anyone, newly grieving, to take even this first step is as difficult as learning to walk for the first time. You are, in fact, back at the beginning of learning to live again, to function, to participate in life. You are learning to live the second part of your life, so be patient with yourself. You're only human. "I can't seem to stop crying, but our minister's wife keeps telling me not to cry because my child is all right now." Well, she's right where your child is concerned, but Jesus wept. Why should we feel too spiritual to weep? Why should we feel guilty when depression swamps us? We're not refusing God's help. It just takes time even for God to get through our sorrow. He formed our minds so that we are able to acquire habits. You are in the habit of having your loved one nearby. Does it make sense that you should simply go on now as though you weren't faced with forming a whole new set of habits?

In that "still, small voice" with which God speaks, He will let you know at some point, perhaps at a moment of helpless weeping, that the next, natural step is—hope. There is no way to bring back the loved one. If we could see him, could see her, in that present joy, we wouldn't even want to bring our loved one back. We can't see the person, but we can begin to concentrate on him/her in a *new* way. Not for long, perhaps, but we can begin. And if we loved, if on earth we really concerned ourselves with the well-being of the loved one, we will find numberless creative things to think about now.

For example: Did your loved one revel in activity? People? Did he or she have an outsized capacity for fun? For merriment? For play? Then, *think*. That person is now able to communicate, to receive, to enjoy, to create, to play, to the fullest, without a single barrier of any kind. All horizons have fallen down. Nothing blocks his or her sense of play or beauty, nothing blocks seeing or feeling or joy. Not even *your* pain, although your loved one is aware of it. He cares, she cares, more deeply than there was energy or sensitivity to care on earth—but at the same moment that your pain is seen and felt, the healing character of God is also seen and felt.

When my father died, Mother said: "Oh, I'm so glad your father doesn't know about the problems I'm having with this house I've bought! He'd be so worried." I thought a minute, and then heard myself answer: "But, Mother, Dad does know all about it. He knows, and because he isn't trapped in time as we are, he knows exactly how God is going to make *use* of what seems to us to be a ghastly problem now. He already knows how it will all turn out!"

Her grief was too fresh then for her to understand even a little bit. Time, which can both trap and free us, has taken care of it now. She does understand that because he is "like God," my father is free to love and care about us here, while knowing exactly what beautifully redemptive thing God will bring out of all that still appears chaos to us.

If Mother had not bought the house, which then seemed such a mistake, she would not now have her two devoted neighbors to care for her. God and my father knew the end from the beginning because they are *not trapped in time*.

Was your life centered around taking care of your loved one? And are you lost now—as though your mission has suddenly ended? "No one needs me anymore." My mother and father worked together. When she lost him, she lost her lover, her companion, and her work. Is it your child who is gone? Are you bereft that you can no longer care for that child? Was your loved one ill? Perhaps old? Helpless without you? Is it still a part of your nature to wonder if he or she is all right? Then, do you almost strangle on the knowledge that you can no longer do anything?

Once more, concentrate on that loved one. Transfer your thoughts—if just for a moment—from your own agony and helplessness to him or to her standing right in the presence of the God who created us all in the first place. Doesn't your loved one need you any longer? Yes. Yes, you are more needed than ever now, but the needs of your loved one have entirely changed. No matter how much you were loved by this person on earth, that person just did not have the capacity to care as now. Your loved one is so full of light and understanding now that his or her need of you is the same as God's need of you. Together, they need you to avoid even the first temptation to feel sorry for yourself. "Why me? Why have I been deprived?" They need you to take what both know is available. Neither expects you to be "just fine" overnight. Both remember what it's like to be in the time trap. But both need you to begin. Your loved one is now participating in the very joy and life of God and is praying that you will not turn your back on God's gift of the "morning" up ahead when joy can come again to you.

Was your loved one a failure on earth by human standards? "I can't stop weeping over her," a mother once told me, "because she died before she ever really succeeded in life. My daughter wasn't pretty or smart or popular. She missed all that life has to offer to most young people."

What about the daughter now? If this mother longed over her child on earth because she was missing what the world calls success and happiness, couldn't that mother be helped by concentrating on the child now—in full possession of all that God has to offer? Free of all human lacks?

Concentrate on your loved one. Did death come before our concept of earthly life had been lived out? It is very easy to say, when an older person dies, "Well, he or she had a long, full life." People shake their heads in bewilderment when death comes to someone young. My beloved old friend Lorah Plemmons died at nearly one hundred and two. We were *not* ready to let her go. My best childhood friend died at age nine when I was age eight. How much difference is there in the eternal scheme of things? Are we really thinking about the person who died? Or are we thinking about our own loss? Both need to be considered.

I cannot fully identify with a parent in the loss of a child, because I've never been a parent. But the hardest part seems to be that the child died so young. Missed so much of human life, of human development. Missed the adventure of becoming an adult. Of course, this is hard for parents left behind, because you longed for your child to have even more than you had. Could our grief be tempered even a little by a more certain acceptance—not a grabbed-for belief in, but an *acceptance* of, the ongoing life with God? The child is not dead in his or her essential being, or Jesus Christ misled us. "I go," He said, "to prepare a place for you; that where I am, there ye may be also." Could any earth joy or adventure compare with what the absent child has up ahead now *with Him*? None of this lessens your pain at missing out on it all, but a true acceptance of the fact of your loved one's continuing life can let in the first sign of dawn.

Your loved one is—in a definite way, right now—pulling for you to make it into "morning."

Concentrate on your loved one. Remember what lacks, what virtues, what joys, what frustrations, were experienced while on earth and be glad for him—for her—now. You can't be glad for your pain. No one is made like that. No one is suggesting it. But I can honestly say that I am glad in behalf of every loved one I've lost. Not glad for the still-sharp missing I endure. *Glad for them.* Life can never, never thwart my adventurous father again. He is where the gift of himself, which he often gave too freely on earth, will always be returned.

Concentrate on the one you miss so keenly. Maybe

it's too soon for lengthy concentration on anything or anyone outside your own pain. But try it.

Everything your loved one longed for or lacked on this earth has now been supplied. Everything he needs to complete him, he now has. Everything she needs, she now has—pressed down and running over. And in the presence of God he or she is praying for you, cheering for you—this minute. That fact can open your heart to its first ray of hope.

Even with a small sign of returning hope, is your pain so intense because you loved so deeply? Where did that love originate? Did it originate in you? In your loved one? If you have just lost your mate, were you able to love that person while you were still together because you learned love from your parents? Did you love because the two of you were so compatible? Shared so many common interests? Did you love because that person knew, above all other persons, how to cause you to feel safe and protected? Did you love your absent loved one because of the way he or she looked? Walked? Listened? Made love to you?

The reasons for loving are endless—and possibly

different with us all. But is any truly the reason you loved? I am sure not. We love—we are capable of love—only because the source of our very lives is Love Himself. "God is love." A vague, farfetched concept at this time in your life? Maybe. But still true. You considered the loved one before you considered yourself—*if* you truly loved. And perhaps some of your pain now is due to self-recrimination because you didn't always consider your loved one before you considered yourself. "I can't forgive myself," a lady in her sixties said to me in the store the other day. "He wanted so much to take a fishing vacation and I put my foot down. Now it's too late. He'd dreamed of those trout streams for months. Now he'll never even see them!"

Wait. This is part of it. Even those who have begun to understand that real love concerns itself first of all with the loved one, suffer these periods of self-recrimination. No one knows how to love perfectly. Which means that everyone endures these times of helpless self-blame when a loved one dies. I rather suspect that the worst part of these times is due to what we call the "awful finality of death." There is now not one thing we can do to compensate. Nothing. Is that true?

Doesn't your absent husband now know you as he was never capable of knowing you on earth no matter how close the relationship? Isn't this understanding like God's now? He not only knows you wholly, he has total self-knowledge, too. Has your grief clouded your common sense to the extent that suddenly your lost beloved has become perfect in your eyes? Undoubtedly you were often selfish. As was he. On earth everyone is human, full of frailties and faults.

If, as with so many widows I know, you did everything anyone could do, your need to go on doing for that person can drive you to seek out someone else who will agree that you did all you could humanly do for the person you have just lost. Above all other things, grief requires honesty—with others and with ourselves. To hear ourselves praised by our friends because of all we did does help. It is human that it should. But that is not what matters now.

What matters now is that we try, with the firmest resolve, to put aside who did what for whom on earth and concentrate on *love* itself. "My husband wasn't good to me, but I loved him." "My wife was jealous and clinging, I guess, but I loved her." "My son caused me nothing but trouble, but I loved him."

"I was sharp-tongued, but he loved me." "I bossed my wife unmercifully, but she loved me anyway."

Love has always been, because God has always been. He is the beginning and the end, alpha and omega. He is also love, so love had no beginning and will never end. God did not merely release the love principle into a troubled, grieving, struggling world. He came Himself, offering all of love to all of us. Love has always been and love is today. Thank heaven, it is understood far more often than we suspect, however imperfectly, by men's standards.

When I was a child, an old couple lived near our summer cottage and everyone, including my family, thought them strange. They conversed in their stoic, mountain way, with us, with neighbors, but almost no one ever heard them speak directly to each other. "Do they love each other?" I asked my mother. Well, they did. One morning the old man found his wife dead beside him in their bed. At her graveside he looked up at the minister and said through tears: "Well, sir, she still loves me. I expect, better than ever, what with the Lord able to help more now."

I've thought a lot about that quaint-sounding

statement. What the old man is telling me now that I'm old enough to understand some of what he said that soft, country afternoon, is that the Lord would no longer have his wife's stubborn streaks or human frailties to contend with. He could get right through to her with His own perfect love. She, in turn, was free in a new, unexplainable way, to love her husband "better than ever."

Gladys Taber once wrote to me: "You and your closest friend, Joyce, should try to learn it well now, that even should one of you die, as my beloved Jill died, love will not die. Whoever leaves simply enters into love as it could not be on earth, no matter how satisfying the friendship was. I began to come alive again after Jill's death only when I realized that she was going right along—in love. And that I could do that, too."

Human love—all human love—whether we are aware of it or not, originates in God. And when even one lover has suddenly escaped earth into God's very presence, still more love can be poured out upon the loved one left behind. Don't pass that statement by as just a "pretty, sentimental thought" to ease the pain of this moment. With no barriers left—no personality quirks, no selfish streaks, no misunderstanding—your loved one is loving you now exactly as you are. With total understanding of the past, the now, the future.

In her beautiful and profound book *Up the Golden Stair* Elizabeth Yates wrote: "If love is the one thing we can be sure of for another who has gone on, and if it is the thing we know we must have while we are here, then love is the link between the known and the unknown, the visible and the invisible. There are no words to convey this. Words can be used only for the known; for the invisible something other than words is required. Yet, has love at its highest, purest, warmest, ever needed words?"

For you now, the instant you can receive it with an open, accepting heart, you will find that new love is being released for you. New love, more love—and it is for you from your loved one. Does something stir in you at the thought of that? Does it perhaps cause more pain, a deeper ache? Well, your very pain is a hopeful sign of life. Life that will ultimately bring you into "morning." Life that can, because it has been carved out more deeply by grief, not only return that love in a new way, but can begin to reach out. To venture a little. Perhaps a very little at first, but where there is life and love, there will be venturing. If the love is real, it does not hug itself to itself.

With God, your loved one is pouring out a new quality of love. And both are cheering for you to begin your venture.

FOUR

*Where Is*
    *Your Loved One?*

*A*bout one A.M. on a July night many years ago, I stood at a quiet, almost deserted hospital nursing station and signed a piece of paper called my father's death certificate.

Off to one side, a short way down the empty corridor, I sensed, more than saw, two orderlies pushing a stretcher cart on which lay a form under a white sheet. Quite quietly, as though I were recognizing some nearly irrelevant fact about the weather, I noted to myself that they were removing the wasted, almost unrecognizable body of the man I had adored since my own life began on this earth. My father himself was not there.

He had called me Chip off and on through the years because I did—except for certain artistic interests—seem to be a "chip off the old block." His block. We were, and I see it more clearly now that I'm nearly his final age, interestingly alike as human beings. We found reason to hope when others despaired. If there was the slightest chance to make merry and enjoy, Dad and I grabbed it. Money, to us both, meant only the means to some happy end, and so neither of us paid it much mind. We were, and I still am, considered foolishly wasteful and overly generous with money. I still hear my father's beautiful laughter as he said, "Don't worry. We'll find more where that came from." We didn't—I still don't—care for dressing up, making a show, and we both hated pretense of any kind. Yet we did as much of that kind of thing as we had to, since we were always dead set on keeping things happy and running smoothly.

Our similarities could fill a book. I mention a few here only to emphasize that as nearly as a parent and child could agree at the center of their beings, my dad and I did. During his long illness with leukemia, I drove hundreds upon hundreds of weary miles, to and from speaking dates, wanting every hour possible with him. To lose him was to miss knowing part of myself.

Rushing through empty, often dark countrysides, usually alone, I had lots of time to think about

Walter Price, the man. Every thought of him then, every thought of him now, is that he was a laughing man, a cheerful man, a man trying through failures and successes—mainly to give joy. He was far from perfect. He seemed almost to have no idea of his own worth. He struck me then and now as one who simply did the best he could, excelling at his profession of dentistry, but paying little attention to his own excellence. He could tell a marvelous story, but he was basically shy. He acted on a whole series of bad judgments in business, but always there was his hope and there was his persistent effort.

As I drove back and forth between my hometown and whatever speaking dates I couldn't manage to cancel or postpone, I had ample time to talk to God about him, to think in God's presence, about the man whose inner drive to find joy had so often been hidden by professional requirements, by the struggle, familiar to me, to be more like other people. By that I think I meant, to be more practical, less of a dreamer, less eager to try anything once. Less foolish in the eyes of others.

For weeks, months, as he endured the illness and its harder-to-endure, quite useless treatment, my pride in him had grown wildly and freely. He wasn't dying a success, as he might have termed it, but he was on his way with truly flying colors. I had become fairly well known then as an author and speaker and had learned to turn an almost deaf ear when I was greeted with: "Oh, you're Eugenia Price!" You see, thanks to my father's cheer and nobility in the midst of his sufferings, I was beginning to be greeted by the hospital staff with: "Oh, you're Dr. Price's daughter!"

My pride in him was at full tide.

Never a churchgoer by nature, he had come, after my conversion, into such a childlike, complete, un-doctrinaire faith in Jesus Christ that he kept me strong through every hour of our ordeal. Nurses roused him every morning at dawn with another needle for still another blood test and he encouraged *them,* lessened their mounting dread of having to stick him one more time. Later in the morning, when Mother or my brother or I walked into his room, he'd give us that grin and say: "Do you know? The Lord came in the window early today and we had the best time."

He couldn't have told you where to find one verse in the Bible. I would swear that the man had no image whatever of himself as a Christian. There had never been, and there never was, a self-righteous thought careening around his mind. He was simply awestruck and delighted with God.

Standing at the nurse's station that night—my name on his death certificate—I found myself smiling as I watched the orderlies and the form on their stretcher-cart vanish around a corner. My father was not there. They were not moving him anywhere.

My laughing, loving, foolishly generous father was not even dead. The real Walter Price—the dreamer, the energetic dreamer—the giver of joy—had simply stepped out that window and into the immediate presence of the God he so delighted in. I have missed him every day of every long year since, but every thought of him is a thought of joy. I still smile when he comes to mind. He did not live a long life and he did not live an unfrustrated life. His dreams were too high for earth realization. Not now. Not as of that minute that long-ago night.

I spoke briefly at his funeral service and I was soundly criticized for it. I was called a "professional religioso" and I was also called hard and unfeeling. I could almost see his smile as the people reacted to me later. His body lay unsmiling below me as I spoke, but *I know he smiled*. The true essence of his life, the real person, was grinning that boyish grin at what they said. Tears ran down my face, but I had seen too much not to let it be known. I had watched the person I loved in a way I'd loved no one else die with the *very joy of God*.

Losing him was harder, of course, for mother than for my brother and me. She had lived with him. But his death increased my load in many ways. Financially, certainly. The long, useless hospitalization (this was before Medicare) emptied the family coffers. But Mother's grief was the heaviest load I'd ever experienced.

Still, after more than twenty years, when my plane is about to land in my hometown airport, a sharp twinge comes—Dad, always standing with that wave and that grin I understood, won't be there. I can't talk to him anymore with that singular oneness we shared—a oneness that sprang from being so much alike that we never had to explain ourselves at all. *But I know he is.*

I can't picture where he is, I have no more sense than you have of its being or not being a place as we understand places. But at long, long last—after a lifetime of striving for it—he is free to express his joy. Free to experience a kind of joy even he hadn't dreamed of on earth.

I know where he is in the sense that I know where

47

God is. And I can't explain that either. No one can. But my father is not dead. He was not snuffed out. He was freed to begin to live fully the joy he had only glimpsed in Jesus Christ while he was on earth with us.

My late editor, Tay Hohoff, knows my dad now. Outwardly, in the limited way earthlings know each other, they would have had little in common. No longer. They both loved me and it comforts me that they can discuss me freely now; can talk to God about me with no human barriers to their access to Him, to their understanding of me. To their understanding of Him. If that strikes you as overly simplistic, I can say only that it goes on comforting me.

When our hearts are broken with grief, God is often the victim of our bitter misunderstanding. How can He be a God of love and allow all this suffering?

C. S. Lewis, when his wife, Joy, died, came honestly close to what men would call "losing his faith." Lewis, the magnificent writer who has undoubtedly opened more thinking minds to faith in God than any other author in history, wrote out of his darkest grief: "Talk to me about the truth of religion and I'll listen gladly. Talk to me about the duty of religion and I'll listen submissively. But don't come talking to me about the consolations of religion or I shall suspect that you don't understand."

If you are in the darkest part of your night now and still unable—or unwilling—to open to the smallest sign of consolation, when all you want is, as Lewis wrote, "The happy past restored"—your rebellion at much that I have written here is to be expected. You, more clearly than those who criticized Lewis for daring to disparage "the consolations of religion," know exactly what he meant. When all you want is the old, happy times back again, you cannot open to any thought of morning.

You want your absent one back where you can touch, share laughter, share meals, argue, look at each other. You don't want to dwell on some nebulous eternity where that loved one lives and experiences a life that may or may not overshadow what you knew together on earth.

A young woman became dear to me through correspondence we kept up during her black, black night of grief at the death—so young—of her dearest friend. In an early letter she told me of having found a note from her friend in the pocket of a jacket. The note read: "Will be right back." The grieving young woman wrote: "Will she? I knew then where she had gone. But, Genie, *where is she now?*"

She is with God. She has entered into all joy. But what does that mean? If my father is free now to be an integral, unfrustrated part of a kind of heavenly joy, that can and does make me glad for him; but what about me? What about Mother, my brother, Joe? How can Dad be so full of joy "where he is" and ignore us, still making our way through human pain and disappointments and trouble? He isn't ignoring us. But if he knows what we're going through, how can he be happy—know joy?

Why should the separation that causes those left behind so much agony be free from pain only for the one who has gone? The answer often is, Because the one you loved so much is in God's hands. My father was in God's hands, too, through all that ghastly suffering: Is he any more in God's hands now that he is dead?

Argument such as this, any attempt to make human logic out of eternal life, usually falls flat. Any attempt to make human logic out of *faith* in any form falls flat. There is simply no logic and no explanation.

Moments come to everyone sooner or later in grief, when for no seeming reason there is a pause in the suffering. Settling into a hot bath, or an almost unintentional glance at a bird flying, or the half-heard sound of familiar voices, may bring a moment of relief. "For an instant," you find yourself thinking, "I almost feel like me again."

Can you explain that?

"God thundereth marvelously with his voice; great things doeth he, *which we cannot comprehend*."

Quite probably—not possibly—probably, we, in our agony, struggle to pull God down to where we are and force Him to explain that which cannot be explained.

C. S. Lewis wrote: "Can a mortal ask questions which God finds unanswerable? Quite easily, I should think. All nonsense questions are unanswerable. How many hours are there in a mile? Is yellow square or round? Probably half the questions we ask—half our great theological and metaphysical problems—are like that."

Beyond even God to answer. Beyond our understanding. The initial leap of faith by which we place our own eternal lives into the care of Jesus Christ is, in relation to getting through our night of grief, no more important than the faith required to leave our loved ones with Him in peace.

Am I wronging the one I loved so dearly by begging God for some answers that will help my pain now? No. Not as we know the meaning of wronging. For the sake of simplicity, could we say that *if* frustration is possible in the ongoing life, we might well be frustrating the one we loved so much?

When we cry out that even our prayers seem directed into a silent vacuum, are we frustrating God?

Frustration, as we experience it, may be nonexistent where your loved one is, but it well may be also that our prayers only *seem* directed into a vacuum. God only *seems* to have slammed the door on us. Our pain, our exhaustion, our shattered emotions, can deafen for a time. If this book has any value at all, it is to remind the grieving heart that God *has promised* a way through the night—and into morning.

When you, by a sheer act of will, place into His hands some heavy trouble that you simply cannot solve, can you explain the relief that often comes? No. Nor can I. If I could entirely explain the marvelous thunder of God, I could not worship him. If I could explain how it is that He "understandeth my thought afar off," I would no longer need such understanding.

Not only in the paralysis of grief, but at other troubled times as well, we do tend to demand answers from God when none is possible.

🦋

Life is a fact. Eternal life is a fact. Extinction is not in the nature of God. He is the Creator of life. Before I became a believer in anything higher than the top of my own head, the blackest horror I experienced was my foolish certainty that one day I would be—extinct. Snuffed out. Dead. Gone. From childhood, I am told, my love of life characterized me. In times of desperation before my conversion, I thought of taking my life. Do you know what stopped me? Life. I couldn't face the thought of extinction. I couldn't face never reading again, never hearing music, never laughing, never weeping. God knew this about me, and so I found a book written by a Trappist monk that convinced me that life after death *does go on*. That there indeed is eternal life. God knew I had to begin there.

Eternal life is a fact or God is cruel to have created in us such a love for life. Eternity, according to some religious groups, will be a scantily populated place. But who are we to decide about these things? We can know that Jesus spoke the truth when He said that ". . . no man cometh to the Father but by me," but how do we know who has turned to Him and who has not? His love, His mercy, cannot possibly be limited to our concept of time or to our semantics. That turning may not have been made in our terminology, or while we were watching or listening, but God understands mere fragments of thought—splintered, pain-filled longings, instants of recognition.

Our faith for ourselves and for our loved ones must be faith in God Himself as we can know Him in His Son. Our faith dare not be placed elsewhere.

When I turned the reins of the wild horses of my life over to Jesus Christ, it was for all eternity that I did it. And, in a sense, I was unable *not* to do it at the moment I realized—began to believe—for the first time that Jesus was right when He said, "I and the Father are one." If God was like Jesus Christ, then I could trust Him with my life now and forever. C. S. Lewis titled his autobiography *Surprised by Joy*. I was "surprised by joy" when my instant of recognition came. When I die and stand in His actual presence—an experience I am not able to comprehend now—I fully expect to be more surprised by even more joy. Surprised that being right there with Him is so much better than merely being at home. And yet I expect to be "at home" as I have never

been on earth. I expect to be surprised that He Himself is so familiar. "So, it was You all the time," the
main character in Lewis's *Screwtape Letters* ex-
claimed when he died and moved into God's presence. "So, it was You all the time!"

Your loved one understands entirely now what
that really means. You can trust your loved one with
Him. Period.

I also expect to be surprised, as the one you loved
undoubtedly still is, at how free we are *with Him.*
Free to be our very best selves. Free in a way the
freest of us are not free on earth. Free to worship
Him face to face—and to work. I could be entirely
wrong, of course, and if I am, something better will
take its place, but I fully expect to work throughout
eternity. In my limited human understanding I can't
imagine *life* without work. I love it so now that I
lack only the energy to do all I'd like to do. But in
the place where your loved one now lives will be
eternal *energy,* too. And perspective. I won't be tired
any longer, nor will I have any of my eccentric blind
spots left. Not one. Jesus said that He is "the light
of the world." Well, He's with your loved one, *who
is now like Him.*

Like God? "We shall be like him, for we shall *see*
him as he is."

"I'm so lonely without him," a professor's wife said, "but my husband had lost his sight. Just think— he can *see* now!"

Yes. By the "light of the world."

Light and energy abound for the one you loved. My own father lay ill for so long, his once muscular body was so wasted, I almost couldn't relate him to the strong, laughing man I loved with all my heart. No longer. He's filled with eternal energy now and able to laugh at all the things that once made him weep.

Try, just for a moment, to *see* your loved one— no longer ill, no longer wasted and tired—bounding with the very energy of God.

Our entrapment in time often limits us to think-ing of eternal life as merely endless. It is, but the quality of that life is what matters. The essence of it. The scope. The God-sensitized capacity of your loved one now to know real awareness of beauty, of love, of praise, of song. Can we imagine this?

No, not really, but we can catch a glimmer: Call up one moment when you were caught—as though time stood still—by the beauty of a single rose. Dur-ing that moment, when indeed time did seem to stand still, you were experiencing a breath of eternal life. We are so worried on earth by so many small and large things, few of us really use the powers of concentration that God created in us. Where your loved one is, there is freedom to concentrate—to be aware. Life in God's presence, I believe, is *total awareness*. When you called up that certain moment in which you glimpsed eternity in your concentrated awareness of that rose, you were not striving to appreciate the beauty—you were caught up by it. The moment held you. Even those who die quickly of heart attacks struggle for a last breath. Perhaps your loved one struggled even longer, but now—oh, joy— *Life* has caught the one you loved. Life Himself holds your loved one; will protect and care for every need forever. Caught and held by Life, by Love, and yet free as we cannot understand freedom.

Eternal life is too vast, too far beyond our comprehension, for us to describe or understand. But it is not shrouded in *too much* mystery for anyone to accept who has ever enjoyed even one hour of human life. I suppose we could select our happiest hour, out time of highest exhilaration, or a meaning-filled period of deep silence and harmony where body and soul and mind did indeed seem to be one. Then we could concentrate on that moment of near

perfection, multiply that joy by *infinity,* and perhaps, just perhaps, we might have some small idea of
the quality, the environment, of eternal life. If there
is need for music, music will be there. If there is need
for praise—we will then know how to praise. If there
is need for work, we will perform it in the very presence of the Creator. If there is need for love—and
there always is—eternal life will be Love living in
our midst. The beloved Christian writer Mrs. Charles
Cowman once assured me that even if I need my
doggie so that I will be complete in eternity, my
doggie will be there, too.

If you loved, if you truly loved, the person you
miss so now, you can find joy in the wonder he or she
is experiencing. Love, you know, always moves
toward the loved one, never away. Love always concerns itself first with what is making the loved one
glad—not with what makes the lover feel safe.

But what, you say, does all this have to do with
that empty chair, that empty bed—a child's empty
room, a silent telephone, that vacant front seat in
the car?

I know, I know how you long to dial a number
and hear that voice again; I know how vacant is the
end of your day when the familiar toot of a horn is
silent. I have experienced the black horror of ringing

a familiar doorbell knowing that my lost friend will never swing wide the door to me again. But, if we love, we can find solace in our loved one's present and eternal joy. If we cannot, if we do not—even for a fleeting moment—we are skirting dangerously close to the edge of *self-pity*.

Even after six years my heart cries out now and then to my beloved late editor. "Where are you? Can you hear me? Can't you help me with this chapter? It's tangled—a mess. Do you really know what I'm going through in my work without you?"

"Oh, I'm sorry," someone said when Tay died, "but you're established as a writer. You'll find another good editor." I wanted to scream. I did inside. Tay was first of all my friend. My loved one. I have not found her again. I don't expect to. I love my present fiction editor equally well, but she doesn't try to take Tay's place. She knows better. She knew Tay. Tay picked her out for me. Tay is still living, eternally. She was not overtly religious, but God and I knew her heart was a child's heart before Him. She is alive and she knows more about me than when she was my "editor dear." She also knows the chaotic changes in our world of books. She knows my struggle to adapt, to change with the radical, revolutionary upheaval in publishing. I'm glad, frankly, that she didn't have to brook this wild tide in her frail, aging humanity. She is now able to take it all in *and* help me. (With all my heart I believe she helps me more now, is more aware of my real needs, than when I could call her or fly to her in an airplane.) I don't understand how she knows, or how it is that she can help, but it is a fact to me. I have the word of God for that. You see, He Himself binds us together—will keep us bound together for all eternity.

Jesus said: "Where I am, there you will be also." My lost loved ones, Tay, my father, my other absent friends, are with Him, and since He also said: "I will not leave you comfortless, I myself will come to you," they are with me, too. *They* are with me? If I believe that the life of God indwells me, and if I believe that my absent loved ones are a part of His life, yes, we are all together.

It would help, oh, how it would help if we could have an actual address, a telephone number, but we have the word of God that this recent, hard good-bye *is* temporary. Nothing hard that happens on earth is forever.

Only eternal life is forever.

You trusted your beloved with your love here on earth. Can't you trust your beloved now—to the love of God?

FIVE

*Venture
into Morning*

"*I* thought you would like to know that today, about five thirty in the morning, the first ray of hope came. Until that moment my grief had spread over everything—like a sky. But in the real sky, today, there was morning light that somehow looked different from all other mornings since my wonderful son was killed. I can't explain it, but the pale gold light, for just an instant, lifted my heart. The relief was only momentary, even though I tried to grab and hold it. But it was there, and now that the darkness has rushed back in, I refuse to let go of the fact of that light."

This grief-stricken young mother had begun her own venture into morning. Oh, I know from my own experience and from the experiences of others that the sun coming up can help for a time. When dawn comes, it means, at least, that one physical night is ending. We can see from our windows again. Unless you live in an isolated spot as I do, traffic begins to move, people appear on the streets going about their daily routines. We feel somehow less alone, less afraid, a bit more able to function than while it was still night. As another friend said when asked if she was managing her grief over her daughter, "Well, in the daytime, I walk around."

During the early, sharp days of grief, even after months have passed and people appear to have forgotten, the coming of day helps. Trees are green and not black as in the night. You can actually watch them green up in the morning light. There is no longer a chance to mistake a familiar bush for danger lurking there in your own yard. The bush is itself again. And on some mornings—not all, but some— you have moments of feeling a touch familiar with yourself again, too. "I found myself actually humming a little tune for a few seconds yesterday morning."

The weeping often endures for such a long, long night that we tend to wonder if we'll ever feel familiar with ourselves again. Feel relief again. Feel free to hum a little tune again. Will the time ever come when we can be greeted at church or at the grocery store or on the street—freely, without embarrassment for our friends? Without their having to wonder because of some look in our eyes, just what to say in the face of such long-lasting grief? Even if moments of relief in the yellow morning light bring what we can recognize as hope, won't the darkness come crashing in again? Yes. Most likely. Night follows day.

But somehow, as long as the sun shines, even as long as we can remember that it is up there shining through an overcast day, the human heart—if it is not bound and locked by self-pity—leaps toward the light.

What is self-pity? Why is self-pity the *only* absolute block to God's activity on our behalf? The answers are so simple, I feel, as to seem ridiculous at first glance: Self-pity clutches itself to itself. Self-pity cannot receive, even from God. Its hands are clenched. God waits for an open heart, an open attitude, unclenched hands. Self-pity turns inward, draws its blinds against the light—shuts out even love. Self-pity cries: "If I can't have the love I lost, I don't want any at all!" Self-pity screams: "Leave me alone. I don't intend to be hurt again like this."

A room can be darkened, even on a sunny day. We control whether or not the shutters are flung wide to whatever light we are ready to receive. Into our rooms, our minds, our hearts.

I once gave a famous lady's autobiography to a grieving widow. It was the story of another widow going on alone. "It didn't help," the woman told me. "If I had her money, I wouldn't be afraid, either!"

"I could come out of this terrible darkness if I had someone left close to me. *She* has children. I have no family."

"I might be able to be myself again—even without my wife—if I had someone to take care of me."

"I see no way for things ever to be the same—not ever! My son was only eighteen when he died. He didn't have a chance to do more than begin to live his life. I'll never see him graduate, never see him married. I'll never have a grandchild at all now. Don't talk to me about what God can do. I won't listen."

Is God's power to heal circumscribed by the nature, the extent, of our grief?

"I have seen his ways, and will heal him." God said that. Did He mean it? Did He mean "her ways," too? Does He skip some of us? Does the God who cares when a sparrow falls to the ground simply overlook some grieving hearts? Does He love some and not all—equally? Are we told that "God so loved the *world* . . ." or are we assured that He loves only His special people and deigns to heal them? Are some tragedies too much for the God who set the stars in place, who bound the seas, and created both you and your loved one who is gone? Is He too busy to bother with you because your sorrow is heavier than someone else's? Too much trouble for Him?

Isn't comparing sorrows, or tragedies, a total waste of time? Aren't we implying that if things were just a bit less stark, we might manage—without God?

Certainly, it is true that some wives who lose husbands seem not to grieve for long, if at all. Some children heave sighs of relief when the troublesome elderly parent dies. But is any of this the point?

Isn't the point God Himself?

Is it ludicrous to believe, really to lay hold of the promises of God—about *anything* that has to do with us? Is it foolish to argue with the psalmist who declared that He had "turned for me my mourning into dancing"? *Dancing?* Is that something you'd expect only a child to believe?

Well, unless Jesus Christ was wrong, to become a child with God is *the* shining key. You say your sorrow is too black, your loneliness too sharp, your empty days too bleak, your nights too dark and too long for common sense ever to accept that the word *dancing* is not madness. But what did Jesus say *had* to happen before we could begin to catch on to the nature of the Kingdom of God? What did He say you and I had to do before we could even begin to make use of His gifts? His words are as simple as they are profound: "Except ye become as *little children,* ye cannot enter the Kingdom of God."

The Kingdom of God is many things. Many more things than anyone knows. But there is one certainty about it: the Kingdom of God is full of *light.* It is full of light—morning light—because the King Himself is there and He is light.

"I am the light of the world. . . ."

"Weeping may endure for a night, but joy cometh in the morning"—*because* "I am the light of the world. . . ."

And He is in this darkness with you. With all of us.

If you are willing, if I am willing, to shun the plague of self-pity, to open heart and mind to the *fact* that God Himself promises the joy of morning, He will lead you, He will lead me, into it. Some

daring personalities can *plunge* with Him into the
morning. Others lag behind, but it is true that He
knows us—you, me—just as we are. Exactly as we
are. "O Lord, thou has searched me and known me.
Thou knowest my downsitting and mine uprising,
thou understandest my thought afar off. Thou compassest my path and my lying down, and art acquainted with all my ways."

He knows every thought that tore at your mind
during the long hours of last night—in the dark. He
knows of the small relief the actual sight of the sun
gave this morning. *He knows you.* And He waits—
with you—never leaving you alone. But He also waits
*for* you, for me, to begin to learn of Him. To learn
of Him as He really is in Jesus Christ. It bears repeating. He is not a quixotic God, not a remote deity,
casting an occasional preoccupied glance our way.
"Lo, I am with you always." With you.

"If only I could *see* Him!"

Here enters the mystery of the necessity of faith.
Faith does not have to be enormous. Jesus mentioned
a mustard seed, almost too tiny to pick up in your
fingers. But, until we are in His presence in the rare-
fied way our loved ones are in His presence now, we
need that living seed of faith. I know of no way to
come by faith other than to do what Jesus urged us

to do: "*Learn of me* . . . and ye shall find rest unto your souls."

And once we have come to see that our every tragedy, as well as our every sin, can be redeemed—shined up, made use of—because of what He is like, we will then not find it so difficult, even in our own dark hours, to believe that ". . . the darkness and the light are both alike to thee."


"Weeping may endure for a night, but joy cometh in the morning."

When is morning? When does the night end? When will the nights be peaceful again? When will I simply go to bed and to sleep—as I once did? When will I feel a surge of hope? When will my night end? When will my morning get here?

It is already morning to God and your loved one. To them it is already morning for you. Remember? They are not trapped in time. They don't wind clocks or set alarms. And through all the seemingly endless hours just past, the very time that has seemed such an enemy has already been used by our Lord in your behalf. He has been tenderly, patiently, quietly, using time to change you. So slowly you may not have noticed, but the first prints of new

69

habits have been forming in your mind. New habits that will serve you in your new life—the next part of your life, which God longs for you to live fully.

Oh, this new life will be different from the old one. The pain of loss never vanishes entirely. Would you want it to? Could you bear the thought of life without the blessing of that relationship? Didn't you learn from it? Didn't you learn a little how to love? How to receive love? Can you think about the potential of this next portion of your life *under-girded* by all that was good in the first?

Grief causes us to feel as though we'd lost part of our very selves. The part of us that belonged to the loved one can no longer be itself. That's true. Love needs an object. But the central essence of the promised "joy" that comes in the morning is that, in a way you *never needed before,* you have been touched by redemption. You feel battered by grief, but in the battering the restoring process was going on, because we belong to a Redeemer God. He can no more help redeeming than He can desert us. His very nature is to redeem, to make whole. In a sense that perhaps you cannot be expected to grasp yet, but that one day you will know, you have been—made new. Deepened. Freed. We fear what we do not know. But now you have known a smashed heart.

And you're still here, aren't you?

Unless you devoutly long for morning, would you still be reading?

Would you still be reading if you had given up all *hope* of morning?

If you didn't somewhere believe that there is a way of getting through the night, would you be reading now?

Is it at all real to you that your loved one is cheering for you? Do you sense a flicker of hope that you can make him or her proud of you—before God? Even if you don't feel you achieved that when the one you loved was still with you, don't forget that that loved one is changed, too, now. He or she is far more able to understand. Your loved one is off his or her own hands and fully into the hands of God now.

"Our God is the great leveler," my father used to say. He knows it now, for certain. Whatever was lacking in your relationship with your lost loved one, it can now have, and in a very real way; and whatever that relationship added to you, the goodness is compounded, because you can begin, this minute, to venture into morning.

And it will be *your* morning. Yours and God's.

※

How can the venture begin?

Actually it has already begun. But, if you are still clutching even a shred of resentment toward God because your loved one is dead, give it to Him as a love gift. A love gift? Yes. He loved you so completely that He takes even resentment, because only He knows how it can poison you.

Death—physical death—is a part of life. Why that's true is mystery, as surely as the need for faith is mystery. You were not singled out by God to be punished when your loved one went away. Perhaps God did not mean for us to die when He first created human beings, but the whole world got twisted on its axis at the point where man and woman began to take authority into their own hands. Nothing has been the same since. Until Christ came, that first Garden, where only beauty and love and harmony reigned, was closed. Now, because His is a Redeemer heart, the gate to the Garden is open again. Forgiven for our headlong deeds of self-assertion (sin), we can find joy in forgiveness, and the same joy at the end of the long night of weeping when a loved one dies.

Your venture into morning has begun. The promise is there—the Light Himself faces you—open-armed, welcoming. Your healing is in His Person. He suffered, so that your suffering can be turned into joy. The kind of joy you didn't dream existed for you or for anyone else.

In an old Bible's footnotes I once discovered that Jesus, when He got up and walked out of His own tomb on that first Easter morning, did not greet Mary Magdalene with "Oh, hail!" The truer translation is that He said: "Oh, joy!"

God Himself longs to rejoice over you. And He will, once you have ventured into your own morning. "He will rejoice over you with singing."

The first step in that venture?

There is no general first step, aside from the willingness to give Him your tears, resentment, and self-pity. But there is a *particular* first step for *you*. My first step into my venture into morning may be something entirely different from yours. How will you know? He will put the idea into your mind. You will decide *how* to carry out that first venture (however timid). You will decide whether or not you will even try it.

My mother, huddled at home on a Sunday morning because she could not face attending church without my father, suddenly felt a compulsion to go to her old Sunday school class and tell them that

God was seeing her through her grief. In no time she was the class teacher and the second part of her life began to take shape. To be meaningful again. She didn't "feel like going" that first Sunday, but she went and that was the first step of her venture into her morning.

A newly widowed young woman told me this story about her own venture:

"Finally, after six months of agony behind drawn curtains, I forced myself to make a pot of my husband's favorite soup. When it was ready, I was still too choked by the pain of knowing that he wouldn't be home to eat it with me, to swallow even one spoonful. Then suddenly, standing in the middle of my kitchen floor, I thought of his mother—alone, too, in her own home across town. In twelve years of married life I had never managed one spontaneous, warm feeling toward that woman! Not before or after he died. I hadn't even called her in all the six months he'd been gone. I might add that she hadn't called me, either. The dislike was mutual. Outside a heavy rain was falling, as it had been all day. There I stood, tears streaming, soup steaming, and what was left of my heart filled with unmitigated ill will toward the woman who had given birth to a man with a heart so defective that he had left me at age forty-one.

"Then my raincoat was on and buttoned up, a scarf around my head, and I was setting the pot of hot, fragrant soup on the floor of my car so it wouldn't spill when I took it to Bob's mother."

The young widow's night was, almost in spite of her, *beginning* to end. The first streak of morning light had begun to break through even as she stood trembling with what she called bitterness and down-right fear—about to ring the doorbell of her mother-in-law's house.

Did her husband's mother greet her with open arms, with tears of joy that their mutual sorrow had united them at last? Not at all. She was barely polite; did not even invite her inside out of the rain to share the soup.

Did the long night close in again for the young widow? No, it did not. I saw a small return of her once delightful sense of humor in her smile. "My mother-in-law and I did not make up. I'm not sure yet how that will occur. I had made one step, any-way. I did what it suddenly and somewhat crazily seemed the right thing for *me* to do. I'm not re-sponsible for her. Only for me. And back in my kitchen, dripping wet, I felt my first real hunger pang since Bob went away."

The last time we talked, there was still no happy ending. Life doesn't always deal in happy endings. But the young widow had, by what seemed a crazy action, devoid of any observable result, left the blackest part of her night behind her. The bowl of cold cereal she ate that evening tasted good.

She had begun—begun, at least—to emerge from her night of weeping.

She had turned *toward* morning. The mother-in-law still has not accepted her, but the local nursing-home staff has, with open arms. She spends every weekend not on the tennis court as when Bob was still there, but gathering flowers from people's gardens in season, slightly wilted ones from florists out of season—and doing her level best to love all the elderly and infirm whose rooms her flowers grace. "I look forward to my visits," she told me, laughing. "It's no big deal." A thoughtful frown creased her forehead. "Do you know, I had no idea there were so many lonely people in this town."

A retired business executive and his wife moved to the island where I live, full of dreams and plans for growing old in the one spot on earth that they both had come to love. They built a lovely home—

just right for them—and began to participate in our community activities and to live. Within a year or so the wife was dead. Norman, his world torn apart, retreated for weeks inside the dream house with his grief. But, together, they had joined a concerned citizens' group we had organized, and one day the thought struck the lonely man that even without her, his life could have purpose. A purpose still directly connected with his love for her, his devotion to their dream. He plunged into the full-time job of attending county commission meetings, planning-board meetings, became president of our group, and for as long as he lived, we, who care about the quality of life and natural beauty of St. Simons Island, had hope of saving it. The gentle, intelligent, diplomatic gentleman entered with all his caring heart into the task of protecting the island he and his wife had loved together. The dream house, once empty and dark, the curtains drawn, was thrown open to group meetings, to consultations with conservationists— to creative activity. Redemptive activity out of which Norman's shattered heart was healed.

"My only son took an accidental overdose of drugs and died." The soft-spoken middle-aged man leaned against a chain-link fence that surrounded the Little League baseball park. "It tore my wife up completely." Tears brimmed in his kind eyes. "In fact, she couldn't stand it. She took her own life." After a moment's effort to compose himself, he added, "I'm sure they're both with the Lord. They were the churchgoers in our family. I didn't go much. But I kind of felt that God was telling me not to crumple up under my load. A few weeks after my wife's death I found myself walking down toward this ball park one evening. Since then I've given all my spare time to helping these kids learn how to shag flies, hit and throw curve balls, run bases." He grinned a little. "Don't know how much I'm helping them, but they sure do help me."

I can hear some of you complain, "Now, don't tell me to get dressed and go out and do something for someone else! I not only don't want to do that, I can't. I'm so dull. In my condition what could I do but drag other people down?"

Undoubtedly, at the blackest point in my own dark night, I'd say—or be tempted to say—the same thing. I fully understand not wanting to be forced to make small talk, to smile, to pretend you are "just fine" when you're anything but fine. And in these pages I have literally prayed *not* to sound preachy. Or even like a teacher. I'm neither. I'm a woman who has also known grief, but who found God in it—working in my behalf, even during the darkest hours of my night of weeping. For me, in my grief, "He made [my] darkness his secret place."

"Shall thy wonders be known in the dark?" the Psalmist asked. Yes. "The darkness and the light are alike to thee." The God of love ministers well to us in the dark. We may be unaware of what He is about, but when the first faint gleam of light urges us to get up, to get out and into the morning, we will discover that, indeed, He has been adding to our inner being, has been shining us up, implanting in us His strength, His concern for someone else whom He also loves.

Actually, your very first step toward morning might be simply to do something you don't absolutely have to do. Anything to move you, however slightly, toward hope. One woman forced herself to bake a chocolate pie. She couldn't eat chocolate and that was the reason she chose it. If she wasn't to waste the delicious creation, she would have to take it to someone else.

It's all right if we go kicking and rebelling into our morning—just so we move.

Gladys Taber, from a point along her own journey

out of the darkness of sorrow, wrote: "It occurred to me, after [my best friend] Jill died, that I suddenly had absolutely no guidance in this undiscovered country of grief. I was just in it. I had faith and prayer, but I really had no training at all." Then, after a time of at least beginning to see the sky and the tree shadows again and to notice what kind of birds flocked to her window feeder, she could add: "Working back into life, I found the greatest guide was friendship. There are two reasons for this: The more I shared the lives of friends, the less I concentrated on my own. The world opened out, wide and interesting. Secondly, I found it eased my heart to spend love (of which I seemed to have a great store). I had time now to make new friends, too, which had not been possible during Jill's illness. And sharing the happiness of others, as well as trying to help with sorrows, gave me a new sense of being a part of life itself.

"I discovered that everyone I knew had room for friendship. The essential loneliness of the human spirit asks for some sharing, even if it be just a casual conversation over tea. And, of course, there is a special affinity between those who have suffered and won through to an adjustment with living. Just the simple words 'I know how it is' may ease someone's sorrow. Perhaps what I am trying to say is that acceptance leads to strength to make new patterns."

Gladys Taber was not suggesting that we substitute other people for our lost loved ones. This would not only skirt dangerously near a foolish, make-believe world; it does not work. The life lived with the one we love was a mass of long-held patterns, habits, ways of doing, of being ourselves together. These patterns are deep in the crevices of our minds. Now, suddenly, the gears have to be shifted. A complete turnaround must be made or we will go on struggling through stifled days that cloak us with dullness—make us uninteresting to other people.

There is no way we can return to participation in those old, comfortable habits of much of a lifetime. We can only accept that fact. Not set our jaws to endure—*accept,* which in itself implies that we mean to begin, at some point, to ready ourselves for morning.

The joy that comes with morning does not always burst upon us in a full, roseate dawn. Sometimes it isn't even watery yellow. Often it is slow, slow, ever so gradual. Our entrance into morning—even our willingness to enter—can come so slowly that we don't realize it is coming until much later. One day, without warning, we may look up suddenly and notice that we've just walked up the stairs to the second floor in the old brisk way. We may notice that the coffee tastes good again. That the bird feeders have been empty for weeks. That closing a business deal gave a hint of the old exhilaration.

Morning does come, and with it the recognition (which may also be slow) of a new kind of joy. This promised joy will not necessarily be related to our old concept of happiness. There is a true difference in kind between joy and happiness. "Joy is God in the marrow of your bones." It can bring times of happiness, but it is joy. Happiness depends upon circumstances. Joy is indestructible.

Joy, real joy—the steady, profound, inner joy that "cometh in the morning" after our night of weeping—is waiting for us to venture into it. We can hang back, we can even refuse, but God will not stop trying to woo us into it. The God who loves us will not stop trying to woo us into at least a careful look toward His kind of creative morning.

When at last we do try to look, there will be all the light we need to see, because He "will never leave us nor forsake us" and He is "the light of the world."

Time, which can seem to be the shadowy enemy while grief is rampant, will show itself to you as having been also a means of moving you toward morning. Even during those periods when you seem to be losing your footing in the loose, frighteningly deep sand of a memory too sharp to allow one more step forward, *time will have been at work for you.* In your behalf. God makes creative, redemptive *use* of everything that concerns us, including time that seems to drag us back and down.

You see, any night does move *through time* to morning. And even in the darkness the God who loves us has been ministering to us without our knowing. It helps if we do know that He has been at work within us through all that black night, but it's all right if we aren't always aware of it. We are human. He is God. And what counts—what gives us the common sense to recognize morning when at last we venture into it—is the fact, the irrevocable, eternal fact, that *He knows us.* And knowing us, returns us to *love,* where we belong.

"O Lord, thou hast searched me, and known me. Thou knowest my downsitting and mine uprising, thou understandest my thought afar off. Thou compassest my path and my lying down and art acquainted with all my ways."

"Weeping may endure for a night, but joy cometh in the morning."

God has given us His word.